THE LITTLE
BOOK OF

DICKIE BIRD

G000146493

Dalesman

First published in Great Britain 2011 by Dalesman Publishing
an imprint of
Country Publications Ltd
The Water Mill, Broughton Hall
Skipton, North Yorkshire BD23 3AG

Text © Dickie Bird 2011

ISBN 978-1-85568-294-8

Printed by in China by Latitude Press Ltd.

The publishers acknowledge the help of Phil Penfold in compiling this book.

Introduction

It's a much over-used phrase, but Dickie Bird is truly a 'national treasure'. Come to think of it, he joins a nice little group of Yorkshire folk who have also achieved that status, among them Dame Judi Dench and Alan Bennett.

When you reveal to colleagues and friends that you are about to meet the man, the reaction is always the same — they break into a smile and say something like "you jammy devil". For with Dickie, what you see is what you get — charming, wryly funny, unfailingly courteous, and blessed with some trenchant opinions. A one-off and a character.

And all of that, I think, comes spilling over in these pages.

Phil Penfold

Whatever I have tackled, I always wanted to be one of the best — and that takes a lot of practice.

The Good Lord gave me a gift, and I hope that I haven't let him down in any way.

Everyone should see the Taj Mahal by moonlight, and everyone should stay at the Taj Hotel in Mumbai. Simply the best hotel in the world.

It's a rare Sunday that you won't find me in church — I'm a Methodist — and I thank the Lord for all his many blessings. If I can't give the Lord an hour or so of my time each week, then that's a poor do.

It's also a rare Sunday when I don't
go out and have a nice lunch
somewhere near my home.

I'm not a great drinker, never have been, but I really do enjoy a couple of glasses of good red wine with that Sunday lunch. Just the two, mind you, never any more.

Green tea is very good for you, helps you in all sorts of ways, so that's what I drink. Just green tea, though, no milk, no sugar. Sometimes I don't even bother taking the bag out of the mug. If you're not drinking it already, start now!

These days, I'm in bed most nights by ten o'clock. It has to be something pretty important to keep me up and awake. A social life is (generally) confined to the daylight hours and very early evenings.

My home near Barnsley dates back to the seventeenth century, and I love every single stone of it. John Wesley, the famous preacher, actually stayed in the house, in 1761, and he slept in my bedroom.

If you saw the view from my garden, you'd realise why I believe in the deity and all his good works. It's magnificent. Stunning. I live at the top of the hill in Staincross, and I can see for, oh, twenty miles, right across the Pennines. Takes my breath away every time I look at it.

Someone once said "It's wise to be nice to folk as you go up the ladder, because you'll inevitably meet them as you come down". I couldn't agree more. What's the point of being rude and discourteous? Bad-mouthing people always rebounds on you.

There are a few things that really get my goat — bad manners is one of them, being rude to old folk is another. When kids these days are rude to their elders and betters, they don't realise that they too are going to be old one day.

Making people smile — now that's a great gift. I love listening to a good story with a funny punchline to the end of it. I used to do a lot of speaking at dinners and 'dos', but I don't any more, not after my illness. It's all too much of a pressure, a strain. But I still like to listen.

It's a wise man who keeps his opinions to himself.

They gave me the Freedom of the Borough of Barnsley, which is an amazing honour — I think that there's only ever been seven or so others who had that given them. I'm told that I can now graze my sheep and cattle (not that I have any) on any public land and on the grass in front of the town hall, and that I am able to inspect any cells or prisons whenever I like, just to make sure that everything is in order. There's not many allowed to do that, eh?

Respect is earned. It isn't given as a right. The world would be a lot better place if some people realised that. You yourself make what you are in the eyes of other men.

Betting is a mugs' game, a total mugs' game. Look at the cars that the bookies arrive in. Very expensive, very flash. You never see a bookie on a bike, do you?

I love the races, don't get me wrong, but I go for the social side, and when I do attend a meeting, there are times when I don't even see a single horse. I'm far too busy enjoying a nice meal and chatting to people to worry about other things.

I once had a racehorse named after me. I was umpiring a match at Canterbury in Kent, and the crowd went berserk when they announced over the tannoy that Dickie Bird had won the 4.30 at Goodwood!

The Dickie Bird Foundation, which aims to help youngsters with their sporting activities, keeps me very very busy indeed. Anyone can apply for a grant, and we listen to everyone. I was a bit surprised when an over-50s football team sent in a request of help, though. Sadly, we had to turn them down!

There's nowt better than the Yorkshire coastline. Words can't describe it. Simply beautiful. All the way from the mouth of the Humber, to Filey, Brid, Scarborough, Robin Hood's Bay and Whitby. Tell me anywhere that can better that?

If you offered me a plane ticket to go anywhere in the world or a rail ticket to Scarborough, I'd choose the ticket to Scarborough. Every time. Nice trip up there, stay in a good hotel, watch a match. Perfection.

Sometimes, you are just in the right place at the right time. Like the day when I was fourteen or so, and I was turned away from a cricket practice. I thought it was all over, before it had even started. And as I walked away, I met a bloke called Alf Broadhead, who turned me round, took me to the nets, encouraged me and my career began. If I hadn't met Alf, well, it doesn't bear thinking about.

Always finish what you've begun. And if you don't think that you can finish a task, don't even start it in the first place.

Stupidest decision of my life? To finish my Yorkshire contract — I felt that I was always being twelfth man, and being sidelined — and to go and play for Leicestershire. My dad told me to stick with Yorkshire, and he was right, I should have done. The things that you do when you're young and foolish, eh?

There's no-one as right as you are
when you're young.

The best cricketer of all time, without a shadow of a doubt, was Garfield Sobers. He was simply magnificent. If someone says that another player, way back in history, was any better, well, all I can say is, I wasn't there to see them, and so I can't make a comment. But I was there to see Sobers, and it was a privilege to be on the same pitch at the same time.

"He was never shy of making tough decisions, and making them decisively."

Sir Garfield Sobers on Dickie

At seventy-eight, I have only one regret, and that's that I never married, and I never had kids. I would like to have had a lad and a lass, and a wife to come home to. But I gave my life to cricket, and the family was not to be. I'd have liked to have seen my children playing sport, as well — at whatever level, it doesn't matter.

Am I lonely? Never. Quite apart from anything else, I've got a whole brainful of memories to think over.

Some of today's sportsmen — and they are mainly footballers — are just in it for the money. Not for the game itself. Many of them have far too much money, and not enough sense. Earning millions a month, and with seven fancy cars in the driveway? Plain daft. You can only drive one car at a time, can't you?

Having looked at a lot of the recent headlines about what today's sportsmen have been getting up to, I've reached the conclusion that some of them would be wise to do a bit more training, a little less clubbing, and to keep their personal equipment inside their shorts.

My mates and I used to play for hours in the streets. Hour after hour, cricket, football, whatever you can think of. The games went on for hours, days, even weeks. I once batted for six weeks before they got me out.

As an umpire, I was so fortunate to go all around the world. I went everywhere, and if I wasn't on the pitch, I was in a plane. These days, I can't stand the sight of an airport. I'm sick of them.

What advice would I give to young players today? Well, it applies to all sports, as much to tennis and swimming as to cricket and football and the rest. And it's this: don't listen to coaches. Develop your own skills and talents, enjoy and understand whatever you're doing. And, when you get to sixteen or seventeen, start listening.

Coaches overdo the natural strengths. Maradona wasn't coached until he was in his late teens. Nor was Best. Or Garfield Sobers or Viv Richards. The list is endless. Those lads didn't do too badly, now, did they?

You can be the most brilliant player
in the world, but if you join
a struggling team, you've got
big problems. A struggling side
is hard work.

You cannot stop change. It's inevitable. Nor can you turn back the clock. Better to shrug your shoulder, put on a smile, and just get on with it.

Why do so many people these days think that it is alright to ride their bikes on the pavements? With no lights, no bell and no consideration for the pedestrians. When I was a lad, a policeman would have fetched you a clip around the ear, and you'd never have done it again.

My motto is simple:
Do as you would be done by.

I am a royalist and a loyalist, and
I am not embarrassed by saying it.
The Queen is a wonderful lady,
and I've met her on countless
occasions. I was once asked to lunch
at Buckingham Palace, and there was
just her, Prince Edward and me.
We talked for hours about cricket
and horseracing and, let me tell you,
the Queen is amazingly informed.
The Queen Mother had me to
Clarence House, as well. What a
charming person.

The Queen was gracious enough to award me an MBE in 1986, and I wear the miniature version of it whenever I am asked out to an official 'do'. I always wear it on Remembrance Day, without fail.

I still do my exercises — every other day, in the bathroom. I believe in keeping as fit as I can, even if the old body is creaking a little bit more than it used to.

It's a sad admission to make, but I don't do the crossword any more. I should, I know, because it's good for the brain. So maybe I'll have to make an effort.

Boredom isn't something that happens to me. I've never had a moment of boredom in my life. There's always something to do, something to watch, something to read. The day hasn't got enough hours.

One of the worst things that ever happened to me was being mugged in the middle of Harare, in Zimbabwe. I had my hand on my wallet, and someone tapped me on the shoulder. Next thing I know, the wallet is on the floor and £500 is missing. All done in a flash. The policeman standing a few yards away had seen nothing.

There are two places other than Yorkshire in this world which I love — India and New Zealand. Beautiful countries and marvellous people.

There's a story that says that I don't like curries. Not so. Light ones I can enjoy, but not the powerful ones, no way. So when I travelled, I always had a lot of fruit that you could peel, like oranges and bananas, and I was never very far from a Mars Bar. Or some chips.

They take their cricket seriously in India. You'd be walking down an ordinary street, and on either side of you, there'd be youngsters playing, often in their bare feet, and with rudimentary bats. It took me back to my own childhood. Playing on the rough is always the best way to train and to develop skills.

The West Indies were once a cricket side to be reckoned with. Now the youngsters over there watch American TV and are more interested in basketball. But the Windies will be back. Everything goes full circle, and they'll be up there once again, alongside India, Sri Lanka and Pakistan.

I'm a proud and very loyal supporter of Barnsley FC, and always have been. I have my season ticket renewed every year. But — no disrespect to the foreign lads — I wish that when I went to watch them, they all came from the town itself, or at least from South Yorkshire.

South Yorkshire is the best place in Britain when it comes to the young football players coming through. There's none that can compare. So why on earth don't we ever play them?

It was a great pleasure to take part in
The Young Ones for the BBC in 2010.
There were six of us oldies, all
well-known in our own fields, and
it was an experiment in coping and
living our lives to the full. Kenneth
Kendall impressed me, as well as
Liz Smith. That gal came in
a wheelchair, and went out on
a single stick.

The saddest words you'll ever hear anyone say are 'If only'.

Jonathan Bairstow of Yorkshire is the young player to watch these days. He'll be in the England side before two years are out, mark my words.

I still get to every Yorkshire match, whenever I can. Perhaps not the whole match, maybe for just a day. But I still love every second of it.

There's not enough humour in the game today; all the pranks and naughtiness seem to have vanished. We used to take the game very seriously — but we had a lot of laughs along the way as well.

The worst prank ever played on me was when Alan Lamb and some of his mates removed the wheels from my car, and propped it up on bricks. Before I found out, he'd even said to me "Have a safe trip home". I could have murdered him at the time, but now I start to laugh just thinking about it.

If tha don't survive the over,
who shall I give them to?

*When Derbyshire batsmen Ashley Walker
handed Dickie his false teeth while batting
on a particularly treacherous wicket*

"Umpire Harold Bird, having a wonderful time, signalling everything in the world, including stopping traffic coming on from behind."

John Arlott

There's very little that gets my waterworks going, but two events moved me a lot: the first was my *This Is Your Life*, and the second was when they raised a statue of me right here in Barnsley. Two very emotional events.

The universities of Sheffield Hallam, Leeds and Huddersfield have been kind and generous enough to award me honorary doctorates for services to cricket, which is a very great honour indeed — especially for a lad who left school at the age of fifteen.

My home is full of things that remind me of my life and my career. I suppose most of my things will end up in museums when I'm gone — I hope that they find some use for them.

What would I save if ever (God forbid!) a fire broke out at my home? My MBE and my three hat-trick World Cup Final medals. I'm very proud of those.

I first opened the innings for Barnsley when I was fifteen years old. The other opener was a lad called Michael Parkinson. I've often wondered what happened to him? Only kidding, Parky!

"I once saw him buckle his pads together so that when he got up to bat he fell flat on his face."

Michael Parkinson remembers Dickie's pre-match nervousness when playing cricket with him for Barnsley

Wherever I am on my travels, I always try and find a church where I can worship. I remember going to one Methodist church in Barbados, and the congregation recognised me, and at the end of the service I just couldn't get away. It was a wonderful feeling — thousands of miles from home, but in the midst of many warm, loving friends.

My dad gave me a sound bit of advice when I was a nipper: "Don't drink, and keep away from the cigs". Well, I only drink in moderation and it's always wine, and I've never ever smoked.

My early ambition was to be both a football player and a cricketer, and a double international. But I crocked my knee in a game (YMCA v Dodworth) when I was fifteen, and my dreams were shattered. I've never kicked a ball since. So, cricket it was.

My name has always helped me,
I think. After all, it's not one that you
can easily forget, can you? I've been
called Dickie ever since I was a lad
in school. My real name? Harold
Dennis Bird, and the last time
anyone called me Harold is lost
in the mists of time.

The vast majority of the people I've worked with and had the pleasure to meet, 99.9% of them, have been wonderful, some of them truly inspirational. There have been one or two, along the way, who haven't been quite so nice. One or two have been totally self-obsessed. I'm not naming names now. I think they know who they are.

Losing with good grace is an art —
and sadly one that seems rather out
of fashion. Better to win, of course,
but graciousness in defeat is a virtue.

If there were an Olympic event for running backwards, I would be the obvious favourite.

If you're going to quit — do it while you are at the top of your game, at the peak of your form.

The team that you can never write off are the Australians. They are completely focused and totally dedicated. As well as competitive and aggressive.

"Look at him. A bag of nerves.
He twitches all the time.
But every Aussie loves him."

Dennis Lillee on Dickie

"I know of very few people in the
cricket world who don't love and
respect the man."

Harry Gration on Dickie

Ian Botham once described me as being "completely bonkers". I didn't know quite how to take that. But then, he also called me "a great bloke and a great umpire", 'n' all, so I've forgiven him.

I wash all my own pots up,
and I make my own bed.
And I hate doing both.

When I start on the chocolate, ooooh, it's terrible. I can eat a full box at a sitting, and it's not something I'm proud of. It's definitely something that I have to watch.

I signed for Yorkshire when I was nineteen years old, but there was no signature involved. It was a gentleman's agreement, and I shook hands with the chairman of the club, a chap called Brian Sellers. Back then, that was all that you needed.

I've lived out of a suitcase since I was nineteen years old — so that's why my home in Barnsley means so much to me.

I once had lunch at Geoff Boycott's home — Fortress Boycott, as I called it. I was expecting some roast beef, maybe, with a Yorkshire pudding or two. What I got was a toasted cheese sandwich.

"That man is respected throughout the world for invariably being firm — but also fair."

Geoffrey Boycott

I am a big believer in cricket, of whatever variety, being played in whites, with a red ball and a white sightscreen.

A few years back, in New Zealand, when each cricketer went out to bat, they played his favourite record, and there was even pop music between the overs! What the heck is it all coming to?

I never had any problem with
any professional cricketer
throughout the cricketing world.

You can have all the God-given ability in the world, but if you aren't mentally strong, then you are going to have big problems.

I've kept everything. I've got it all on shelves, in cases, and framed. So many happy memories. It'll be the local museums and Lord's who get it all in the end. If they want any of it.

Match souvenirs? I admit that I have been known to switch the stumps before the end of play, and taken one to my dressing room as a memento.

Over the years I've had more white caps stolen as souvenirs than I care to count. And I also gave a lot away to be auctioned for charities. That raised a lot of money over the years, I am very proud to say.

"An outstanding ambassador on behalf of our country."

Lord Mason of Barnsley

After my retirement, I had a lot of proposals of marriage from the ladies. I politely turned them all down. My sister Marjorie advised me that it wouldn't work, and that I was "too set in my ways". She was, of course, right.

My belief is that there ought to be total commitment in a marriage — and I could never have offered that.

I didn't mind flying that much, but I am lousy on a boat. Really queasy. In fact, I'm so bad that one fit of sea-sickness happened while I was out in a little craft in the middle of the lake at Peasholm Park in Scarborough. And that's not even a couple of feet deep!

Train journeys always fascinate me ... wonderful scenery rolling past, often someone interesting to talk to, and — on occasion — listening to someone else's conversation. Like Alan Bennett, I'm a great eavesdropper.

"…loved for his eccentricities and his sense of humour. The game was never dull when Dickie was umpiring."

Former Prime Minister John Major

Apart from a cricket ball once hitting me right in the place where it would hurt the most (and believe me it did!) the most pain I've ever been in came when I was judging a caged birds show in Birmingham, and a cockatoo bit me on the nose. There was blood all over the place and then it swore at me. The second word was '–off'.

The main problem when I was umpiring? Intimidation. No doubt about that whatsoever. I could not have lived with my conscience if I had let intimidation get out of hand. Any threat of it and I would pounce.

The secret of umpiring? There's no 'secret', all you have to be is fair — and consistent.

Money isn't everything. Principles are far better. I know, I'm the man who turned down an 'offer you can't refuse' from Kerry Packer. How much? I'm not saying, but I never would have worried about a bill landing on the mat again.

I loathed apartheid and all it stood for. Loathed it with a vengeance. It doesn't matter to me if someone is black, white, yellow, or green with pink dots. If someone wants to see a game of cricket, they should be allowed to do so.

Those of us who are readily recognised, and in the public eye, have a huge responsibility for furthering that sport and its image. No exceptions, no excuses.

It's been sad to see so many divorces in sport, where couples have grown apart because one or the other has been living or working away from home.

Snakes and I don't see eye to eye.
I'm terrified of them. And
considering that I've spent a lot
of time in India, Pakistan and
Australia...

"He is a great umpire — not because he does not make mistakes, but because of his integrity and his wonderful nature. He recognises that players are human beings and not robots."

Imran Khan

Watch myself umpiring? No, I never ever did. Not on the edited highlights, nor on any of the news programmes in the evening. No 'action replays'. If I had, I think that by now I'd have gone crackers, and would be securely locked up somewhere nice and safe.

I take no notice of replays. I never look at them. My decisions have been made as I've seen them at the time, and then I stand by them.

"He has become such a national monument that I was going to suggest that Dickie should eventually be mounted, stuffed and displayed in the Lord's pavilion, but I suspect that he might object to this."

HRH The Prince of Wales

Some TV folk once suggested that I did an interview with Lily Savage — in bed with her. I did it sitting in a chair. I wasn't having any of that nonsense!

It's entirely possible that one day a Test umpire will break my record of 159 internationals. They're going to be damned tired when they do!

They asked me on to *Desert Island Discs* once — I think that a lot of people were a bit surprised at my choice of records. The one I'd take with me if I could only pick one? Barbra Streisand singing *The Way We Were*. My book had to be *Wisden's Almanac*, didn't it!

In sport, one sex is no better than
the other. Just different.

Women play a pretty mean game of cricket — those at the top possess incredible ability.

Freddie Trueman, who I respected enormously, rated Wilfred Rhodes, the former Yorkshire and England all-rounder, the best of all time. I don't know how he came up with that one — he admitted to me that he never saw him play.

I've got to admit that I had my doubts about one-day cricket when it came in in the early 1960s. Would it take off? But it did, and there's no stopping it now.

I was looked after wonderfully when I had my stroke, in 2009. The doctors, nurses, carers … all marvellous. But I have to say that it's my belief that a lot of the pills that the doctors prescribe you should be flushed down the toilet when they leave the room.

When that stroke happened,
I couldn't move my right side, my
mouth was all skewed, and I couldn't
write … it was terrible, I wouldn't
wish it on anyone. But I prayed, and
I prayed hard. And He must have
listened, because here I am. So yes,
I *do* believe in miracles.

The worst thing about that stroke was that I lost all confidence in myself. And, after my prayers were answered, it slowly but surely returned. Another reason to believe.

When I had the stroke, one of the worst things was not being able to write for a while. That's all come back now — and I've even got permission to drive again. I've always loved my driving — but I'm uneasy when someone else is doing it and I am the passenger.

I would ban all running on hard surfaces, indoors or out. When I watch a jogger going past, I know in my heart of hearts that physios and orthopaedic surgeons will never be out of business.

I wish I'd had the time to take up golf — and I would have wanted to have been a really good player, because I never do anything by halves.

My favourite word?
Determination.

The bit of umpiring advice that sticks in my mind came from Jack Crapp, who had played for Gloucestershire, and who was on the list when I first started. When I asked him for his advice, he told me "Young man, pack it in". I'd hardly even started. But I learned later that he said that to everyone. I'm glad I didn't take it.

Other books published by Dalesman:

The Little Book of Yorkshire
The Little Book of Yorkshire Humour
The Little Book of Yorkshire Dialect
The Little Book of Yorkshire Christmas
The Little Book of Lancashire
The Little Book of the Lake District
The Little Book of Country Sayings
Harry Gration's Yorkshire Sporting Heroes

For a full list of our books, calendars,
DVDs, videos and magazines,
visit www.dalesman.co.uk.